WRITTEN IN STONE

WRITTEN IN STONE

Poems

M.C. St.Clair

CvR-StC Fine Art

for those who love words
yet long to transcend them

CONTENTS

AVALANCHE

LIGHT LIKE THIS

"Art must be an expression of love
or it is nothing."

— MARC CHAGALL

AN ORCHESTRA OF SENSES

.

WRITTEN IN STONE

Imagine night voices
circling a crackling fire
whispering narratives
that move
through the arguments of day
howling
gurgling
clucking
feral storytellers
sharing each adventure
with a huff
a sigh
the impossible whoosh of a nighthawk
no words
no punctuated stops
no obstructed breath

In contrast, these markings
on cream-colored paper and bound into a book
scare me. As soon as the letters settle in,
they fix themselves to the page and refuse to budge.
They employ explosive consonants to surround
breathy vowels, locking them in and forcing them
to comply with unambiguous meanings.

When printed, words can lose their vitality.
They can become rigid, inanimate, insisting
on impressing, manipulating, convincing a reader
to follow their lead. Even the inspiring ones can feel
like rules. Preachy. Off-putting. Insincere.

I want to shrink away from all this.
To stay silent and protect my vulnerable vowels.
I want to become the observer.
The observed.

But I'm a lover of words
struggling to use this language I misuse,
this language I long to understand.
I want to hold it like a brush, to reach
into the pigment of my brain, to stroke
what I touch in my dreams, to offer a voice
to the murmur of humus beneath my feet,
to a willow's dance,
to a distant mountain's moan.

How ironic, this work
of setting
every
syllable
in
stone.

THE MOVE

I miss the grinding holes
at the edge of the stream
behind our old home.
I miss the Upper Truckee River,
my daily swims with our pup.
Beavers, mallards, owls.
The occasional golden eagle.
I miss the meadow of wildflowers
surrounding our decks. Acres
of mule's ears, columbines,
lupines, corn lilies.
I miss the jagged mountains
right outside our door.
Bears in the alpenglow.
Cougars in the heavy snow.
Marmots in the sun.
Mushrooms in the fall.
I miss the solitude.

We bought a house in Truckee.
Cozy. With a perfect art studio.
We have to walk through a neighborhood now
before finding water.
We must travel far before we can disappear
into the wilderness. Yes,
we do spot coyotes, raccoons, and
every once in a while, a porcupine.

Show us how to live here,
I urge the listening part of myself.

This is how I process change.

If we offer the best seeds,
red crossbills might visit our yard,
and flying squirrels.

If we plant a healthy garden,
native swallowtails might appear,
and yellow-faced bumble bees.

If we bend our ears to the earth
—just maybe, if we're patient—
an ancient river might sing to us
about waterfalls
cleansing our assumptions
and pounding rocks
carrying stories
of those who once lived here.

Remember us, they say.
Follow the tributaries to come.

SHE THINKS LIKE A FOREST

When she walks through a forest,
she senses the talkative trees,
the silent ones,
the seedlings seeking attention,
the sick who shrink away.
Now and then she turns, places hands on bark.
She knows the tree can feel her skin
and detect her shoulder's droop.
It lets her lean against it.
Invites her to sit.

Sometimes when she rests there,
she feels the earth breathe beneath her body.
The inhalation may be soft, easy.
The exhale a soundless sigh.
Nearby boulders heave
with ancient tears.
She doesn't hear them with her ears.
When she rises, the soles
of her feet inform her.
Now and then she turns,
places hands on granite,
touches the whisperings.

HOLDING A SPOT IN THE SKY

Last night I followed the flight
of a Western Tanager from Central
America to the Sierra. Their nests
squirmed with foreign chicks.
Far below me, I saw forests burn
around cities spreading like cancer.
I woke with a start.
Only then did I know how to paint
this yellow bird.

When I was asked to paint a bear,
I prayed for a dream. I ate salmon
for the first time in decades. I went to bed
filled with expectation. Nothing came.
No image. Not even the slightest hint
or shadow followed me into morning.
I paced in the studio. Rearranged my paints.
Even cleaned the bathroom. Still,
no trace of a dream.
Until this:
A slight tingling in my hands.
A straightening in my spine.
A bolt of warmth through my fingertips.
When I lifted my brush,
a bear
ran across the canvas.

Some of my best paintings
come from dreams.
Is this too bold to say?

I once dreamed of a storyteller
listening to children who asked
for a tale to heal the earth.
One child shook his head.
The earth doesn't need healing.
We do.

Today, three paintings
join forces in my Truckee home.
The Western Tanager.
The Bear.
The Storyteller.
Together, like constellations,
I picture them soaring away
from my artist trappings, and

holding a spot in the sky
to protect our sacred planet

from each other,
from ourselves.

Washo Country

They say mountains like these
actually breathe.

The gray seed plants are ready
to harvest

when you catch them
chatting in the desert winds.

If you look with your other eyes
you can read the language

of the landscape. They say
if you're very, very still,

you can hear the ancestors
weep.

Her Hands Carry the Scent of Endless Autumns

We sit like dolls carefully placed,
backs supported by a stone wall,
legs extended flat against the sand.
We laugh and turn, sink our toes
into the warmth, and face the necklace
of mountains hugging the lake.

She takes a stick and draws
patterns for her next baskets,
sharing the dream
that allowed her to see them.
Water lulls our words to rhythms,
quieting us for long spaces.
We squint at *Da-ow-a-ga,*
the lake of her ancestors.

I talk about clouds, eclipses, comets.
She shares stories of her grandfather.

We plop on our bellies, marveling at ants
clearing pathways over the cliffs
of our fingers. She traces circles
that move grains of sand away
from the center and back again.
My fingers add more circles. They mingle
with bits of dried leaves, punctuating
their connections.

Her hands carry the scent
of endless autumns.

Gatherer's hands
selecting roots and herbs for healing,
collecting gray seeds
and pine nuts for soups.

Hunter's hands
scraping and curing hides,
twisting rabbit pelts into long ropes
that wait like promises
to be woven into blankets.

Forester's hands
grafting limbs broken in winter's wake,
nurturing seedlings into hearty trees.

Artist's hands
praising her heritage as she weaves
fern roots with willow branches she splits
with her teeth.

A mother's hands
speaking of her sons, bringing them
up to grow wise and strong.
In balance.

Hers are the hands of a friend.
She takes mine. She lifts my face
so my eyes can meet her smile.

We shake sand from our clothes
and walk to our waiting cars.
The sunset cleanses us.
Our hugs are forever.

Tomorrow,
she will give her presentations,
sharing *Wa'siw* ways.

Today,
I want to keep her here.
I want her people to return
to Lake Tahoe. Call it home again.

Um-na'wa.
Me'mle.
La'ka.
Your land.
Your heart.
One.

Yé.

Broken Language

The storm shrouded you well last night.
Stiff peaks of gray and gold shimmer
beneath the snow. My fingers smooth
the crick in your ear. The weight
of my hand leaves a depression
in your crystallized fur.

Once one of your cousins followed me.
I turned into his golden stare
while two others circled behind. Rotating
with them, I tried to remember
their language.

My neighbor once found a coyote like you
draped over the back seat of his car.
Stained red.
Practical joke.
Strange language.

I separate the fur surrounding
the circular wound in your neck, touch
your frozen nose. I wish I could use my voice
to soothe your spirit.
But my language is broken,

and the crack
of the gun
still echoes
through the trees.

WINTER NEWS

Everything repeats.
Snowed-in-driveways.
Frozen windshields.
Screaming fan belts.

Again and again,
we see each other at the post office.
Exchange smiles.
Massage mittened hands.
Muse between letters
about the latest front mounting the summit.

Whatever lives beneath the surface
seldom rises. Instead, it lingers
near the doorway of our lips.
Hesitates.
Retreats.

VENUS

It's my favorite, the Cheshire moon.
And above it—what planet is that?

"Venus," he says, turning me around
and pointing to a different section of sky.
His flashlight, a highway of floating particles,
reveals Delphinus, Cygnus, Aquila.
"Do you see them?"

I hear his voice, but I'm still thinking
about Venus winking above the crescent moon.

My mother winked like that.
I called her a goddess
while rotating her withering body,
taking care not to break her
smile. "Here comes the sun," she sang,
urging me to join her chorus
of fragile moments.

Spontaneous lyrics
cracked my voice.
Little darling.
My mother.
My universe of stars.

I bathed her empty body
with scented oils
and waited
for the men with the gurney,
the zipped bag.

I miss her, my mother goddess of love.

It's late. He presses his mouth to my ear.
"Little darling," he whispers and circles
me back to the tiny planet
teasing the grieving moon.
He aims his flashlight.

"She's still here.
See?"

Autumn News
after Arthur Sze

A man stacks irregular rounds of oak
against the side of his house.

A woman listens to the squeal
of tires being replaced in the shop.

A child opens and closes his fist
over a wadded piece of white bread.

Pachelbel's Canon skips
in the CD player.

A nuthatch slips off its perch
while trying to crack an oilseed on a branch.

A dog drags the lower half
of a deer back from the reservoir.

A squirrel tugs on a half-frozen towel
left outside in the yard.

Skid marks on I-80 swerve around a pile of logs,
over the centerline and into a scattering of glass.

A boy draws a picture of a dragon
eating his teacher.

A girl sharpens her pencil and writes
I love Mario in her notebook.

I rest my hand on your thigh.
You push your hands into fingerless gloves,

pull arm warmers up your sleeves,
and hop on your bike.

I open a book
and watch a yellow aspen leaf fall to the floor.

Window of Invulnerability

You promised to show me how to bend a note
the way Howlin' Wolf did with his late-night
hoodoo that made everybody cry. You promised
to introduce me to Sugar Blue, who packs
his harps in an ammunition belt
strapped across his chest.
You promised me glissandi, trills,
clusters, chords. You wanted me
to ache to take a breath.

Listen to James Cotton, you said
the day before you died. You opened
your leather case, sifted
through a dozen harmonicas
until you found your favorite key.
That's when you told me about the window
of invulnerability, how you had to crawl
through it before you could learn about life
and death. Only then
would your right ear separate from your skull
and hang on your cheek, searching
for a new way to hear.

You put the harp to your lips and blew
away your time in Vietnam,
the day your first wife left you,
all the empty bottles you broke on stage.
Those long nights after gigs
when you awoke to static on TV.
You turned all your sins,
hooked them, wrestled them,

morphed them into moon-shattering blues.
"Juke," "Whammer Jammer," "Stoop Down #39."
Never argue over the song.
Passion.
That's the only thing that matters.

This is how you bend a note, you said.
You use your tongue, your palate, your throat.
You reach deep into the hollow and grab
the sound. Wrench it into your gut, real slow,
all the way to the underbelly of your being.
You squeeze it out,
every breath of it,
until you're
crawling
on your knees
begging
for
one
last
riff.

His Cigarette Voice Burns Holes through Fog
for Floyd Salas

Feet stomping shoes.
Green confusion under soles.
Designs glazed with colored
lines in shapeless faces.

His cigarette voice burns holes through fog.
Fisted arms punctuate the air.
Rough, featherweight
images smoke the room.
He jabs
hooks
slices
stings
runs two-step (heels slap floor).
Women.
He flashes a smile.
A wad of paper in his back pocket.
See? It's all here! Never leaves me!
Bukowski fire
in pacing syllables.

Screwdrivers.
Floating cowboys.
Silver eyes like fish.
Benches. Cocks. Sawmills.
Swanky horses.
Mistresses!
Wicked narwhals and dying unicorns
in tides of touching spring.

Write it down! Don't wait
for time-studded hours
while armored symphonies wade
through conductive waters.
It's free, man!
Free of limitation.
Free of accessible lies.
Threads of music before time.

A poet's truth.

Thimble Hall: A Daydream

Daddy sold it to a butcher in the thirties.
Said it didn't mean much since Grandad died.

That bit of a cottage almost kept the damp
from creeping in, all those foggy mornings
when Grandad rang the tin bell on his bike.
He must have been ninety then. I remember
that grin he gave us before slipping out
while Gramum snored from the spring bed in the loft.
His bell meant berries from Muffett's Farm
and fresh Duncan cream. All us kids, we'd pile
out of our blankets, run to the window, and watch
the wind lift cobwebs of Grandad's hair.
He'd be all shivering beneath that bare sweater.
Gramum meant to mend it, but yarn and thimbles
were scarce those days. Still, he'd be glowing
his crooked teeth inside that smile just the same.

Mummy and Daddy were in California
carving a spot for us someplace warm.
But Grandad's shivering never stopped,
and Gramum's followed. All us kids, we sat
at the window, waiting for America.

My granddaughter showed me the picture
in the paper. They're selling it again,
Thimble Hall. They say it's the smallest house
in Britain. Detached. Bleak. Shrunken.
A holiday spot in a park, it is. £15,000!
Now that will buy a lot of thimbles and yarn
to mend the cold.

JUMP ROPE

Carl on one end.
Amber on the other.
Turning ropes tap pavement.
Maria moves her hands in a trance,
checks her rhythm, darts
through swinging openings.
Angelica follows. Cat and Mouse.
Carl tightens his grip.
Maria bounds again.

Angelica, tiny Angelica.
Her breath draws in
the way the world does in winter.
Her eyes mirror the beating ropes.
Sunlight dances across her face.
Soon, she'll be a flutter of wings,

and Carl will remember her name.

An Orchestra of Senses

When I lift my brush in the wake of it,
at the height of crescendo,
I can dive into the song head first.
Liquid rhythms, full-bodied, vibrate
through pooling waters.
Reflections.
A dip of pigment.

Choruses swirl
through me. Voice-waves
urge my fingers to choose
sienna to honor this tree.
Roots carry the river's song.
Branches stretch the tone.
Soprano sky.
Baritoning trunk.
Tenors of duff.
Harmonizing melodies
beneath textures of soil.
In unison, they sing.

I'm going deaf, the doctor tells me.
His glasses reflect the blues
in my brown eyes, the crooked bridge
of my nose. I can't imagine
a world without my favorite songs.
Frogs, chickadees, crickets. Distant
coyotes. The scrape of charcoal
across cold-pressed paper.
My husband's voice,
his whispered words at night.

Will the lack of sound
guide my nose to even more
perfumed glazes? My eyes
to deeper shadows and surprising light?
Will it sensitize my tongue
to flavors of accomplishment
as I clean my tools? Will it weed out
my endless complaints?

I listen to the hum of the doctor's voice,
the deep tone of a bow
vibrating across a cello's strings.
Ultramarine. Alizarine crimson. Naples yellow.
Arias cresting,
pools of promising pigment.
Spaces.
Images expanding.
Rolling arpeggios texturing each stroke.

In the end, he says,
a drumming will take me.
Serenading hues will fade
before they flush clear.
My palette will no longer hold
the colors of music.

What do I know
about silence?

What do I know
about my singing soul?

PRIVILEGED PROTEST

STILL

There are people we don't know,
people we've never seen in our neighborhood,
walking strange dogs that trigger
our border collie who notices
every out-of-order detail. Still,

the number of Covid cases
in our tourist town
has remained steady these last few days,
despite the surge in second homeowners
vacationing in place. Still,

the chickadees fly
away from the odd
bird seed we had to buy.
Like us, they prefer the old ways.
My husband and I argue
about venturing out,
whether it's safe
to get toilet paper. Still,

the Cassin's finches chow down.
They love this other stuff, wonder
why we never offered it before. Still,

I'm tired
of this cough, this
invisible spike stuck
in my throat, this
haunting aura of fever. Still,

the neighborhood howls
each night at 8:00, partying
on behalf of the nurses,
the clerks, the mail carriers,
the drivers, the EMTs still

working their butts off
so strangers can walk their bewildered dogs
and mine can count how many canine steps
she will have to take to reach the edge
of the driveway, and sheltering locals
like me can thank these heroes from the inside
while watching houseplants
in their resilience, in their strength,
in their silence,
demonstrate how easy
it can be
to stay

still.

BLUE

I thought I knew blue.
It was once a rich pool
I could lift with my brush
to accent a feeling.

It was the long hour before sunset,
the base of a Bunsen flame,
the pudgy face of a second full moon.
It described me
on nights when even a good book
couldn't soften my fears.
Dreadful blue, I called it,
until it faded into morning.

Today, blue is the flat part
of my friend's right eye
after laser burn.
It's the ashen light
stuttering in my living room,
holding me captive, flashing images
of satisfied couples and mud-splashed
four-wheel drives. It's a naked emperor,
cobalt, like the tip of my tongue
after blackberries and fudge.

Flickering images of politicians
say there will be no more blue.
Blue is now red, they say,
and I believe them.

PONDERING NOVEMBER 22, 1963,
APRIL 4, AND JUNE 6, 1968

After the assassinations, we spoke
against injustice, marched with strangers,
bled in the streets, in the jungles, and
while working to protect endangered people,
endangered species, endangered cultures,
endangered habitats, our endangered world.
We fought for clean water, solar energy, electric cars.
We were students, waiters, janitors, clerks.
Secretaries, assembly workers, cab drivers, maids.
We sat behind desks, delivered newspapers,
and picked fruit in the fields.

We created music, art, poetry.
We sang.
We dedicated our lives to abstractions
with hollow names: equality, justice, truth.

To say we failed is to admit
we're descendants of those who came before us.
Our parents suffered the Depression, the Holocaust,
World War II, the Bomb, the Japanese internment camps.
Our grandparents grew victory gardens, sold war
bonds, distributed pamphlets, sent sons to the front.
Our great-grandparents fought slavery and lost
family in the Civil War. Generations suffered tyrants
who demanded loyalty, spread lies, eroded trust,
silenced dissent, toppled institutions,
and decimated populations who got in their way.

Our skin is in this world.

We didn't quash cruelty in the sixties,
not because we didn't care or try.
We failed because despots don't go away.
They simply rebrand.

WHILE WATCHING *LAUREL CANYON* ON TV

In the midst of the scene
where the nude woman in a mental hospital
talks about shame, I hear it.
A backfiring car making its way toward town.
Or is it someone setting off fireworks near Prosser?

My thoughts turn to the Santa Cruz Mountains
where bullets used to sing overhead. Tiny projectiles
protected a neighbor's patch of illegal green.
At the same time and place, another neighbor lost
his mind, decades ago, in Vietnam
and triggered a gun to his head.

Tonight, the sound is more
a pop than a zing. Followed by a series of pops,
then silence. Then another round
of children huddled in school closets,
of families and lovers hiding
behind grocery store counters,
seats in crowded theatres,
playing dead
in synagogues, mosques, airports,
and *Laurel Canyon*.

Disgrace
is no longer on the lips of the naked woman
in the movie. She turns her back.
She walks away.

MAMA SAYS
after the Shirelles and every other "Mama Says" poem

Mama says words are lies. She says poems like this sound like stream-of-consciousness-journal-spew we did as kids. Writing we hailed before learning about writing. Stuff we crammed into our heads before the world got hold of us and twisted every ounce of innocence from our anemic, anorexic, self-conscious cells. We've become social media posts hoping for the comment that will tell us we're finally worth something in this pumped-up-look-at-me world.
Rip cellophane, tap the pack, suck it in, exhale into slam-bang-cool faces jazzed up to rap volume, and go back sixty years—
booze club
sax
black turtleneck, baby,
lose it all for me.
Today, losing it all means taking cover behind tinted windows, earth-scarring SUVs, five-hundred-dollar-bleached-and-torn blue jeans, micro-brews, finger on the head-banger-punk-rap hide-in-the-clouds pulse, half-finished screenplays spilling from suede briefcases, gaslighting newscasters, rocket flashes, demolished towns, election fraud, gun violence. Person. Woman. Man. Camera. TV.
All for clicks.

"Words are lies," Mama says.
"Didn't you learn nothin' in school?"

GRIMM

I once read about a dragon
who collected paintings, books, flutes
(like all good dragons did in their day).
He knew the names of things.
He could recite sonnets, sing arias,
quote dates, and recall periods of greatness.

Then one morning, he awoke
and questioned the things he loved.
It was wrong, of course. So wrong
the higher dragons turned him
into a human being
as punishment.

The old creature fell under a strange spell.
Blue light flickered on a tiny screen.
He held it in his hands and watched
newscasters mime tradition,
monster pickups gouge wounds
through wetlands,
children being shattered
by bullets
in classrooms.

He ate popcorn while watching
an actor slash another actor's neck.
Made jokes when a father slapped a son.
Pixelated images numbed him,
and he never asked why.

Then he typed out words.

Waited for comments.
Became angry.
Typed out more words.

This same dragon once cared
about prodigies bowing
La Rigolade on small violins.
He'd relished the Grand Adagio,
read plays by Euripides,
wept while viewing Poussin's
Echo and Narcissus.

Today he's buried
himself in digital rubble.
War-torn. Exhausted,
Clicking on memes,
Clicking on more.

I want to shake his shoulders,
bring him outside,
whisper in his ear,

Look up.
Take a breath.
Remember where you came from.
Remember who you are.

See This Mountain?

It's a big playground now
with two gigantic holes
blasted clear through it.
A place to plant dollars,
kick rocks out of the way.

Do you remember
when this mountain was a place
of worship? And this cave?
This cave where a wise man
came for visions
so he could help his people recover?
This cave where a young boy's uncle
received the Ways
and sang them to his children?
This cave where a healer
noticed a drowning child
and dove through frigid waters
to rescue him?

Do you remember
when this mountain was sacred?

Battles were won
and lost
here. Ancient fighters lie trapped
beneath the surface of the People's Lake.
There was a time
when you could hear the mountain
breathe for them.

Not anymore.
Hallowed ground
no longer suits us.
Grafitti and disrespect
are what we indulge in now.
Here.
There.
Everywhere.

THIRTY-SEVEN DAYS

until the election. Thirty-seven chances
to ask for courage so I can climb
out of my political dread.

I hide.
Cover my panic with pretty words.
Bind myself to my drawing table
where I can conjure dreams with India ink,
a fountain pen, an overused
sketchbook with a broken spine.

I don't hear the public alert, warning
of a man on the loose. My phone
is on mute. I can't find it.
I don't even know where to look.
I imagine the intruder entering my house
while I'm busy tossing socks from drawers,
searching for that stupid cellphone.
Do I startle? Or run? Or grab a book?
Do I open the book? Or throw it at his face?
Do I even notice if he has a face?
Or if he is a she?

A catastrophe, these thirty-seven days.
My slow burn changes shape,
hour-by-hour, week-by-week,
reflecting silly fears
about what has not yet occurred.
Assumptions kill me.
Even as I vote.
Even as I live.

Polling Place

Candidates cast their votes, stroll
down hallways, wear soundbite smiles.

They look me in the eye,
but they don't see me.

I sign the register.
A man inks a red check beside my name.

Halloween candy in a jar.
How quickly holidays fade.

Garbage bag curtains shield the booth.
Plastic clings to my shoulder.

I doodle in the margins
of my sample ballot. It takes a while

before I blacken predetermined bubbles.
In the hallway, a child cries.

WEDNESDAY

I know what I couldn't have imagined this morning
while sipping tea and sitting on the porch, watching
squirrels thump their feet at the dog and
grosbeaks quarrel at the feeder.

At school, a fire ignited the kids' voices.
They told me details I didn't want to hear.
How he shot a girl in the face.
How the victims and gunmen could be
any one of them in a class like this.

Now an angry wind pushes my car.
Unexpected downpour. Rain
cracks against the windshield,
fierce as the fury in today's classroom.

Safe at home, I insulate myself.
No TV.
No Internet.
No phone.
No black coffee staining an opened newspaper.

I sink into the womb of my hemorrhaging brain
and listen
to the rain. The howling wind. My longing
for unremarkable days.

Split

WAR IS A CANVAS PAINTED BY FEAR.
—*ANONYMOUS*

We still don't get it, the hairline
between hope and fear.
At ten, he held his promise high
as he ran across the ballfield.
A kid. Gangly. Potential
is like that. Too soon,
his pudgy chin grew strong and hard.
Home from the war. Jaws clenched. He begged for a fight.
She loved him anyway. Typical
in stories like this.

When it's your story, though,
the "typical" part becomes irrelevant,
absurd even. But they didn't see it

that way. They opened their eyes to each other
and the daily struggle. Nothing else
presented itself. Flies buzzed around undone
dishes. Too much sweat, saliva. They no longer hoped
the way you and I do. Slippery thing,
fear. In time, their emotions congealed
into a clot of confusion. Confusion replaced reason.
Helplessness set in. At that last moment,
who was around to hold them back?
He held the gun. She pulled the trigger.
In an instant, they fell.

Pain does this. It's our story, too.

Eleven Guides

Too quickly, everything changes.
You think you have time to prepare,
yet you don't prepare
because deep inside there's a voice
that says, "This isn't real. Fascism can never happen
here. In our neighborhood. In our country. Not to us."
It's a pretend preparation, a default option,
this impossible reach toward normality.

We were given this world. You see this now.

Coyote
Raven
Coopers Hawk
Three who guide you as you walk.

Coot
Dragonfly
Bald Eagle
Three who meet you at the river's bank.

Turkey vulture
Chipmunk
Deer
Three who take you into the woods.

Junco and Chickadee
greet you at your door,
their calls, urgent for seed.

Eleven guides.

And their helpers:
Douglas fir
Jeffrey pine
Ponderosa
Cottonwood
Aspen

Feed us, they say.
Feed us now.

FOUR ACTS FOR VICTIMS AND SURVIVORS

I. Night Noise

She's a small woman
trapped
her wailing reduced to a feral call.
Deep in the mountains,
pinned beneath the weight
of a drunken man.
Echoes in dark places.
Just a night noise, he says,
one hand tightening her back,
the other silencing the tongue in her mouth.

II. Chains

shackle his hands and ankles. Locks
anchor him to the chair.
This is the second time
I identify this man
without meeting his eyes.
Scarred white rivers
flow down his forearm.

Before. The white glassed room. My finger
trembling, singling out the man on the edge
of the line. Manicured attorneys. Burnished
briefcases. Wooden stares. Men shuffling papers.
All
men.

Now. Courtroom chatter. Black suits.
Orange prison pajamas. They say
he buried her parts along a foggy
woodland path. Evening. Jogging.
What was she wearing?
Men carrying flashlights, polished badges,
deaf to her cries.
And to mine.

III. Stranger on the Bus

Let me show you my scar,
he says, parting his shirt wide.
A jagged gash crosses his heart.
No one else will listen.

Even after I close my eyes,
I see that jogging woman,
her fleshy tear. In my mind,
I change the course of things,
turn the knife's flash,
mend the broken shadows.

IV. Vocabulary

My sister says being a victim
is like having wings. You learn early
to fly away from your body.
I'm thinking of V-words.
Venus. Victory. reVenge.

We no longer wear short skirts,
skimpy blouses. Sometimes you pay
for things in unforeseen ways.

"There's no such thing as a gentle
man," my other sister says.
Viper. Voyeur. Vermin.

We search the dictionary for
a different V-word.
Vasectomy. Vaseline. Verbigeration.

Vulnerable Vixen in Vizards
aVoiding Voluptuous Vampires.
We roll on the floor.
Laughter
streaks our faces.

Volkswagens.
That's it!
A way to get away.
It must be.
We each have one.

FLYING SQUIRRELS

It's late. I'm depleted, exhausted, depressed.
The nightly news scares me.
I wonder if I have it in me

to do something good in this world.
Like making life easier
for these nocturnal creatures,

immense and aware,
with expanding universes for eyes.
Despite the bobcat waiting below,

despite our desperately barking dog,
despite the screen door slam,
they soar from the nearest limb,

wrap their winged bodies around the feeder,
and make this place their home.
Does this mean we don't have to

pack our stuff and move to Canada?
Ignore the plight of the country
and leave our loved ones behind?

To be watched by flying squirrels is a joy for me.
To be watched by me is a threat to them.
Still, they stay.

PRIVILEGED PROTEST

The keys we hunt for.
The zippered pocket we find them in.
The trendy vest that holds the pocket

filled with keys that open doors
to expensive rooms with hickory floors
and solid roofs. Full pantries. Refrigerator

lists. Energy bars. Eco water-bottles.
Power T-shirts. Yoga leggings.
Backpacks carrying constellations

of gum wrappers, earbuds, stainless
steel straws, designer sunglasses,
individual packets of sunscreen.

We tie our silver laces. Step out
in brand-name athletic shoes
with custom orthotics. Simple

things. We betray ourselves
with our privileged protest.
We march because we can

walk away
without being seen.

AVALANCHE

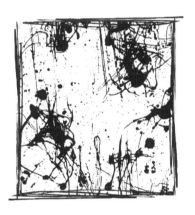

At the Crossroads: Wildfire

A thick veil of smoke transforms the landscape
into an impressionistic painting. I wait
at the red light, search the glovebox for a pen,
and begin a poem about fire.

But I'm distracted by the flames
stitched across the shoulders
of a girl's leather jacket. She guns
her Harley's engine in the lane

next to mine. Light hair pulled into a braid,
black cord plaited through blonde weaves.
On a bike beside her, someone else
has the same thick braid, the same black cord

lacing through it, the same flames
sewn on dark leather. Broad shoulders
and scraggly beard tell me he's male.
Are they twins?

The light changes. Their bikes
bellow through falling ash. I'm astonished
by their metaphoric relationship
to the burning hills I've tucked away

in a transient part of my brain
to think about later,
after the bikers fade into the painting
and the red sun returns.

MY COUSIN AND IRA GLASS

When I look at this picture of Ira Glass,
I see my cousin
dripping with lake water,
slamming the screen door.
He skates across black
and white linoleum squares
to the refrigerator.

Skinny little kid
wearing dark-rimmed glasses.
Believes everything we say.
There's a little man turning the gears
on the motor on top of the fridge.
Wanna see?
My oldest sister teases him.
It takes three of us to lift him,
he wiggles so much.

Gramma has one of those ice boxes on four legs
with a chrome latch. The motor on top
is bigger than all the bottles of Pepsi inside.
It's gray. It gurgles. It spits.
My cousin's big glasses are now glued
to a small opening in the steel casing.

"I don't see the little man," he says.
Look harder.
"I'm looking!"
His sagging shorts soak our T-shirts.
Sixty pounds suddenly becomes six hundred.

The little man must be taking a break, my sister says.
We'll try again later.

"No! Wait! It's him!
Now I see the little man!"

At twenty-one, my cousin still has that innocent face.
Dark rims. Ira Glass's voice.
Meditation books and maps
of Arkansas litter Gramma's kitchen table.
We discuss Karma over Pepsi. Gramma's
bruised arms. Her black eye. Holes
my cousin punched through the wall.
He buries his head in his hands.

Nobody talks
about him anymore.
Not after a neighbor found him
face down on a pile of rifles
in an Arkansas trailer
deep in the woods.

On summer afternoons, while listening
to *This American Life,* I pretend my cousin is still alive
as Ira's twin with double-pierced ears
sharing his childhood story about a little man
cranking an old refrigerator motor
to keep the sodas cold.
I can't help it. In my heart
I hold the little boy in him, the kid
trying to save face after being picked on
by three giggling sisters
who thought they were just having fun.

CONTROLLED GROWTH
An Elegy for Truckee

While driving down Highway 89
from Sierraville to Truckee,
a coyote jumps into my car.
He whines, howls, lifts his forepaws to beg.
I happen to have a bag of coyote food with me,
so I feed him.

We travel together, snacking and pointing
at the moon. Suddenly, a great horned owl
flies through the open window,
hooting and carrying on. I grab a bag
of owl food from the glove box
and feed her, too.

The three of us continue along the road
until a large doe leaps into the car.
I give her deer food I keep
in the back seat for times like this
and reassure the coyote he'll be well-fed
so he doesn't have to eat the deer.

Just then a flying squirrel swings through
the skylight. I lean down, fumble under my seat,
pull out a sack of squirrel food, all the while
convincing the owl she'll have plenty
so she won't have to shred the squirrel.

We munch our way along 89,
getting closer and closer to Truckee,
when suddenly, the front tire explodes,

exhales, sinks to the pavement.
Stunned silence.
Furry
feathery
frozen
fear.

I flip hazard lights, search the car
for lug wrench and jack
and discover
to my horror

we've eaten
all
the food.

TAKEN BY WATER
for Gary and Tina
in memory of Dugald Bremner

Tina's drowning!
Looking everywhere through the reef,
you can't find her. You jerk your head
above the waves, rip off your mask,
scan the waters.

Five paddlers stay in your house
while you're in Mexico. One, a photographer,
extreme kayaker, back from a first descent in Russia.
Dugald, your friend since school. On assignment
for National Geographic.

You wake with a start.
Humid air, hotel blankets tell you where you are.
Sliding your hand beneath the sheets,
you find your wife by your side.

They try to lift Dugald out by his vest.
It comes loose.
By his helmet.
It snaps.
Water rushes over them, knocking two men
into the river. One grabs onto a branch, pulls
himself out. The other, rescued by the extended leg
of the man holding Dugald's hand.

You and Tina return home.
Something's wrong.
All your messages blur into three words:
I'm so sorry.

Six days later, the county can't get Dugald out.
Too dangerous. He'll have to stay
in the river till September.
You resist. Phone Colorado. The best
in the business. Winches, ropes, infrastructure.
Thirty people with specific duties. Rigged
up for the official day. Sheriffs, politicians.
Watching
with binoculars.

Two hours of daylight left.
Thumbs up.
Everyone works quickly,
one entity with many arms.
Half an hour of daylight left.
You finally pull the wedged kayak
and your friend
from his frigid grave.

He seems to come alive,
slips through your hands,
floats downstream.
Unified and calm, rescuers
retrieve him in the twilight.

Dugald's fiancée counts his fingers,
trying not to dwell on the last time he touched her.
You hold space near the rock where she sits,
his body in her arms.

You zip the bag, tie it to the litter.
Tina scales the mountainside above,
talks with waiting parents, siblings.
Rescuers struggle through darkness.
Precious cargo.

A flashlight reveals the side of his face
in the opened bag. During the journey uphill,
he's somehow turned onto his stomach,
his best profile illuminated.

That's how he always slept,
whispers his mother.
"Just   like   that."

RIVERS

The Upper Truckee River flows under our house.
We straddle the floor heater and listen
to the water sing beneath our feet.
Outside, snow falls. Silent. A foot an hour.
If we don't get out there soon,
it will consume the first story.
Yet here we stand, mesmerized
by underground songs.

I feel the swell, the flow,
the frozen droplets accumulating on the windowsill.
Outside, grinding holes lie buried
beneath centuries of seasons like this,
of women squatting on the boulder
overlooking the bank,
preparing for what's to come.

Tonight a new river rushes through me.
It's dark. After midnight. In the bathtub
I submerge my screaming body and pretend
I'm a fish, a mass of primitive cells
releasing someone I love,
someone I ached to save.

To lose a child is like drowning.

Water gives life.
Water carries it away.

SURGICAL RESIDUE

A thin red line bisects my belly.
Each time I close my eyes, I leave my body
and hover over this strange woman shrieking
through a black tunnel. Howler
Monkey. Mountain Lion.
Her screams are barely human.

An acupuncturist pinches a fold
of skin between my eyebrows.
Inserts a pin. "There," she says,
"You won't think so much now."
Legs, forearms, two points
just above the scar, she thrusts needles
everywhere it hurts.

In a cedar chair on the porch, I watch
nuthatches and siskins argue over perches.
Chickarees spiral up the white fir
and pause to drum warnings.
Pillow tight against my middle.
Blanket. Slippers. Electrolytes
in my glass. A month. Two months. Three.
Reserved
for breathing.
Graduating from beet juice
to baby food
to vegetable soup.

Listening.
Lifting a pen.
Dropping it.

If You Dream of Fish

If you dream of a stream,
you might be wondering how
your life is moving.
If fish are in the stream,
you might be diving
deeper.

Yesterday, someone told a boy at school
he looked like a girl, so he shaved
his head and asked if I liked his haircut.
He trusted me to tell the truth.
I lied.
I loved his long hair, the face it framed.
Now he seemed exposed, unaccustomed
to the cold.

Today, he cried in front of class
as he read his poem about a fish
lost in the ocean
with sharks all around.

If you dream of fish,
you might be breathing water
through gills you had before you were born.
A simple organism, like countless others,
struggling to survive a shark-infested world.

If you dream of a boy with peach fuzz hair
swimming with bullies in that school,
can you keep their voices
from destroying him?

BREMEN

Princesses are sweeter than prom queens,
you said, pinning a tiara in my hair.
Barely seventeen, I relished those words.

I spent days covering your guitar
case with millions of painted dots.
Seurat electrons dancing
in the shape of a rose. You held
that case high before boarding the plane.
Follow me to Bremen!
Your kiss caught the wind and flew
past my cheek. I turned away.

In your Black Forest kitchen,
I chopped onions. You cracked eggs
in the pan. After breakfast, you took
my hand. We left the room's
lacy light, an old rocker casting
shadows across the floor.
You spread a blanket near the river,
pressed my palm to your chest.
I cupped my hands to catch the flow
but couldn't hold your words.

I imagined a slippered old man in that rocker.
Stale darkness beneath thatched rooftops.
I saw myself as an old woman stirring turnips
and beets in copper pots, throwing scraps to storks
and Bremen-town musicians.

At what point does a princess lose her sweetness?

I seal the envelope,
not expecting a reply. But here it is,
postmarked high on the lip of Germany,
taped with chords from your songs
and pictures of me
standing beside you on the podium,
thorny roses in my arms.

Of the Wild Horses

Bill Graham used to be Wulf Grajonca,
when he was spirited away to an orphanage
before his mother died at Auschwitz.
Dusty Springfield's original name
was Mary Isobel Catherine Bernadette O'Brien
in her early days as an Irish immigrant.
Peter Coyote was a Cohon
before his first peyote trip.

You might say I stole van Rossem from a can
of Rotterdam tobacco. I pictured a wild boy
galloping between windmills. I wanted that
name so bad. When I was fifteen, I wrote it
in the margins of my math book. It graced
the inside of my binder with spiral flourishes
in red ink. I scribbled it
a million times on scraps of paper,
tucked them into my blouse.

Each of my father's daughters traded
his Puritan name for someone else's.
He celebrated freedom. For himself,
but not his girls. Of the Wild Horses?
Too reckless for his youngest child.
He'd rather I stayed a White a while longer.

In defiance, I slipped into my feral name.
On lucky days, it fit. I showed it off, pranced
around like the wild Konik who gave it to me.
Then I yearned for something quieter.
A name to lighten my worries, to inspire my dreams.

I added a "hee" to my feline signature
and a Saint to its tail.
Not as English as White
nor as unruly as van Rossem.
It's something sacred
to gentle me.

*

---

* Polish Koniks are horses that run wild in some regions of the Netherlands.

69

VIOLIN

His fingers flew across the strings.
Bow arched and swayed, right arm a blur.
My father never told me he played the violin.

At the 1960 Olympics, after Carol Heiss won
the gold, Dad tied laces on our skates
while Mom darted across that frozen pond,
hands clasped behind her back.
She never told me she was a speed skater.

I thought I knew them,
these strangers in my house
who drove my sister and me to school
and scolded us when we didn't clean our rooms.

Black case. Fire velvet interior.
Small doors hiding resin, cloth.
I unpacked my tiny violin,
tightened the bow until it bounced across the strings,
attended to the arc of my wrist.
I copied my father's frown, his down-turned chin.
Stretching my fingers to reach the highest notes,
I mimicked the pain of music.
Fragile meadow.
Frogs trilling.
Flowers opening.
Bees tuning chords in the sun.
I savored the urge, the thrust
of my palm's heel pulling
the bow from its base, awkwardly
crossing the bridge.

My mother waved as she waited on the other side
of the pond, skateguards in her hands.
My hockey-playing father joined her.

I didn't know what to do
with my parents' dreams.
As a fifth grader, I was already a tangle
of taught strings.

They called for my sister and me.
We wavered.
She march-pushed across the ice.
I strained to stand on the edge
of a narrow blade.

Speed Skater

Her white hair glows like a halo
as she scales glaciers in the Bugaboos,
ice tips on her crutches.

She knows exactly how to arc
each fused ankle
over intimidating boulders

and still keep her balance. In her mind,
she's shaving frost with her blades,
cutting a clean line into a frozen lake,

lacing her mittened fingers
behind her back, then swinging them
wide with each stroke.

I was nine when I first saw her skate.
Before I could adjust my laces,
she'd already disappeared across the ice.

Now I'm a painter considering her face,
the furrows in her forehead, her child-like smile,
her full, uncertain chin.

Ice, blade. Water, brush.
Mother. Daughter.
We could be opposites. We could be twins.

SURRENDER

Somewhere in Africa, women are fleshy
and large, their soft strength admired.
No symptoms of heart disease or menopause
exist among these grand matriarchs.
Their legends tell them
Age Is Status. Sexuality Fills Both Hands.
Regal women in colorful cloth
wrapped around breasts, tucked below bellies.
They move like oceans.

We share lunch. Musicians, dancers, artists.
Our conversation takes spirited twists.
I do not understand this land,
says the storyteller, his voice clicking in valleys
and peaks. *Women look like men here.*
And men enjoy seeing their own reflections
in the bodies of their women.

In Nigeria, Efik women sit in fattening rooms
created for their beauty. In mud-and-thatch
houses, they eat bowl after bowl of rice,
yams, plantains, beans, and cassava.
They learn about childbearing
while making cradles of their hips.
An honored rite of passage.

Here, we teach girls to become addicted
to thin, to put their fingers down their throats,
to fit into impossible clothes.

We surrender to a different god.

To My Sisters

I have on my desktop a folder called "Grief."
Through the years, I've filled it with writings
to help me crawl through this dark tunnel.
A fable about a snake.
Essays on gratitude and loss.
Meditations (loving-kindness).
Poems.
Way too many links,
way too many opinions.
What speaks to me may not speak to you.

Still, we share the same fallen tree. Snags
catch us unaware,
especially when we think we're aware
of all the rain burdening our branches.
Mudslides trap our roots. Water helps us grow.

Times are good when we see each other and smile.
Sunshine. Rainbows. Blue skies.
But it isn't wise to believe only rainbows exist, so
we go back to slogging.

These are our gifts:
To stumble. To look up. To smile.
To climb. To fall. To curse.
To nurse broken connections.

We're tired. Angry-tired.
Sobbing-tired. Giving-up tired.
Yet we rise.

There's a phrase I love. It's repeated again
and again in the I Ching: *No blame.*
I ink it into my palm
in Sharpie. Black ink
bleeds into the dry lines of my skin.
On my other palm, I write
Compassion. An overused word. It runs over
the side of my left hand because my right
has a hard time containing it.

We are not victims. Nor villains.
We are unambiguously human.
Refugees fleeing our own ruins.
The route is rough.
We keep going.

No blame.

THE WRONG MUSE

1.
Our mahogany Buddha laughs
from the kitchen windowsill.
It came all the way from China.
A Mafia lord gave it to a relative
who represented him in a court trial.
This transformed Siddhartha
was sent to watch over us.
To balance the energies,
I tape a quote by Thich Nhat Hanh
above the sink. About water
flowing over our hands,
helping us to do good in this world.

2.
The other day, I ran across a book by an old friend,
skipped stairs to share his holographic theories
with Greig, who was running
apples and bananas through the blender
beneath the watchful eyes of our Buddha.
I imagined having lunch with David Bohm,
watching him fold
and unfold
paper napkins.
He described the cosmos,
the implicate and explicate orders.
Particles. Waves. Macroscopic worlds
resting on microscopic worlds.
I pictured God playing
leapfrog with the universe.
Dr. Bohm folded his napkin again.

3.
My gallery show will be here soon.
Instead of painting, I collect words
to transport me through unchartered realms.
My grandfather loved words, too.
When he lost his new set of teeth in the lake,
I dove too deep for my breath
several times
before finally surfacing
with his voice in my hand.

4.
Fifty-some years ago, my college professor
questioned what I'd do
if I only had six months to live.
(Probably wouldn't finish any paintings.)
What is time, anyway?
Something we've invented
to worry us through the truth of things?

5.
Here are several canvases to complete.
They stare at me, like this wooden Buddha,
while I distract myself on the keyboard.
Maybe I've summoned the wrong muse.
Painting is about getting noise out of the head.
Writing charms endless utterances to rise
like cobras from my mental pit. Given too much
attention, language hypnotizes. Overpowers.
Paralyzes an artist's hands.

6.
If I had a deadline to compose this poem,
I'd be at my easel now.

AVALANCHE

My foot is swollen from a spider bite,
yet I still walk with my friend and listen
as she tells me about the avalanche.
I live the details of her story
and feel a monumental weight.
The roar consuming her, the taste of pitch-dark fear.
It's a heavy space, an endless void without dreams.

She speaks of pain, of crushed bones,
of the arduous task of healing.
But mostly she talks about
her friends. Those she'd lost that day.
What is death but a welcoming by lost friends?

I consider the throbbing welt below my ankle.
My pain is easy compared to hers.
But death? I still can't grasp it.
Is it a graduation? A celebration? A moving on
after combing through life's tangled chapters?

I ask my friend what would happen if we never stopped
saying their names, safeguarding their stories,
honoring their dreams—would it be possible
to become the ones we've lost?

We both nod.
This is what love is.
Perhaps it's what death is, too.

LIGHT LIKE THIS

MRS. DUMPTY AFTER THE ACCIDENT

A disease it was, his sport.
The only thing that ever split us up.
Once I asked him to quit.
He raised those white brows, cocked his head a bit.
I didn't bring it up again.

I never wanted him to climb The Wall.

He and his buddies'd go out
training every day.
When the deadline finally came,
twelve of them chickened out.
Not Hump, though.
He wouldn't give nothin' up.

I knew something was wrong that morning.
With rope and carabiners strapped to his middle,
he got his gear all tangled. Couldn't find
those silly shoes. And he leaned a bit
too far
to the left.

It's something every poor wife dreads.
The nurse movin' her head so slow.
They're missing a large piece of him, I'm afraid.

Then there's this girl
runnin' around town spreadin' rumors
about the surgeon's dog eatin' breakfast
in the operating room.

Tight Jeaned Julie with a Hook in her Forehead

Gotta be careful fly fishing with Mike.
He has a loose wrist.
Windy days are the worst.

More than a breeze teased the waters
on their first fishing date.
He wanted to impress her.

Tied his favorite red humpy
especially for that trip.
Even polished the old metal boat.

She took a delicate position
on the seat behind him. Buffed
her nails as he arced his line.

His barbed hook bit deep
between her sweet sable brows.
Utter surprise choked her voice.

She couldn't say anything,
even at the hospital
when he almost touched

the blue dolphin band-aid
swelling like a wave
on her forehead.

Dating Italian Men

Two guys in a red Fiat take the dirt
road to the Big Farmhouse.
They've heard about us,
twenty American hippies
living on a countess's estate.

Ponytails tight against their skulls,
thigh-hugging jeans, leather jackets.
They slam the car door James Dean style,
swagger to the iron knocker.
Mary and I call from the window,
Vieni a insegnarci l'italiano? Bravissimo!
You come to teach us Italian, right?
Before they can answer, we take
them inside, seat them at the table,

place paper and pencils before them.
All afternoon, we conjugate verbs:
Io sono, tu sei, egli è, noi siamo, voi siete.
The two tire of the game.

Raimondo grabs my arm. Gianni shoves
Mary into the tiny car. Raimondo drives. I clutch
the dash as we burn up and down narrow hilltown roads,
slide through snowy fields, spin
to a halt before a failing fence.

Raimondo touches my face, resumes his lessons:
faccia (face), *naso* (nose), *carina* (cute),
occi (eyes), *bella* (beautiful), *boca* (mouth),
b-a-c-c-i-o (kiss).

Gianni rolls up the windows, secures
the corners of a red plaid blanket to separate
front seat from back. Raimondo whispers,
"madly in love," "must kiss," "agony."
He's willing to forget girlfriends
in Perugia, Rome, Florence,
and in his apartment,
for just one, juicy, sensuous, warm—

I nail him hard on his sprouting *mento* (chin).
A storm rages
as we make our way back to the farmhouse.
Raimondo and Gianni in the front seat now,
nasos to the windshield.
They get out of the car Charlie Brown style.
Raimondo stomps powder from his boots.
Mary and I climb from the back.
Gianni scowls, targets us with wads of snow.

They return the next day, oddly renewed,
John Wayne hats on their heads. Looking
for hippie chicks. You know,
the real ones.

JUAN'S GRANDFATHER

He's a tiny man.
Smile as wide as an arrow's bow
arcs across his face.
Shy hands hide in deep pockets
as if to reach for invisible treasures
far beneath his knees. Two curious toes
bubble through worn socks
attached to restless feet that rock
back and forth. Clothes fit loosely.
Sweater unravels here and there.
Looking up, the man nods,
Buenos Dias.
His grin broadens until his face
is nearly swallowed by it.

Juan wrote a poem at school
and sent it with this affectionate
rendering of his grandfather
on the surface of a fragile eggshell.

Mi mensaje al mundo
es que niños y abuelos siempre ser juntos.

A young boy's longing
to be with a lonely man in Mexico
who waits
for his family
to return.

A Glimpse of Truth

He leans back in his chair, chews
on a pencil, crosses
knee over knee and watches
from a distant corner of the gallery.
Somewhere in the meat of his muscles
rests the essence of a mountain.

He doesn't hear his patrons
engaging in colorful discussions
about the spot of crimson in his painting,
how it appears to mate with viridian in the rock.
Instead, this artist slips away,
calls his family on a static-filled phone,
inquires about his son's loose tooth.

If I were to catch a glimpse of truth,
I might find it somewhere
on his crowded palette
or mingling with his worn brushes.
It might lie beneath layers of Damar varnish
or woven between the fibers of stretched linen.
It could take cover behind stacks of frames
or in the pages of his sketchbook, hidden
within thumbnail studies of mountain lions and lilies.
Perhaps it's waiting in the hues, the values, the shapes

—or yes! I see it now, in the lines
of his smiling face as he steals
a moment away from the crowded gallery
to joke on the phone
with his little boy.

BLACKSMITH

This hang-gliding man hammers fire, bends steel,
twists black metal into rams' horns,
dragon's tongues, and creatures from Mordor.
Our home is blessed with his creations.

His work would weigh him down if it weren't for his wings.
Last week he flew with a flock of geese. They fell
behind him in formation, asked him to be their leader
for a while. Now, whenever I see waterbirds in the sky,
I hear metal clanging against anvil
and picture their chatty beaks
silhouetted in his flame.

That same red blaze once shaped a bowl for me.
When I coaxed its rim with a stick, songs
of molten rivers flowed from ancient caves.
He said the chords sounded like
calls from an aerie of eaglets.

Today, he won't be at his forge. A raptor
has just taken flight. With wings
strapped to his arms, he catches
thermals with the osprey, who must think
this human curious, he soars so close.

Blackened strength in feathering fervency—
this is how I will paint him. Firelit face. Muscles
flexing with the weight of the hammer.
His touch will be gentle.
His bellows will voice a zephyr's cry.

BETWEEN THOUGHTS

It doesn't come from words.
It comes from a pattern between thoughts.
An awakening. A current
running up the spine and into your heart.
A pulsing rhythm
sending trailers through your fingertips.

An aspen tree flutters in response.
Yellow leaves dance in the sun.

You need this energy
to connect, to survive.

To be an artist is to ride the obstacle of thought
until it dissolves into an allowing.
Once the fire begins to move,
there's no stopping it. Dawn animates.
Washes of ultramarine, naphthol crimson,
cadmium yellow evolve into a passion-filled sky.

Let it be, you whisper when the trance is over.

There are no teachings in this process.
To be an artist is to disappear.

WINE TASTING

Consider a knight, secure
in his shield of armor.
He could be the zin in her glass.
Rich, from the queen's court.
Royal alizarin, her favorite color.
She slowly releases him,
bolt by bolt. A patient search
for the heat of his breath,
his quickening pulse.
The scent of fresh meadows,
strange blossoms. Her lips
dip into nectar, ripening plums.
A tapestry warming her throat.
First passion.

Her second taste is acrid.
Coarse salt pushes forward,
puckering her mouth. Dark purple
screens her eyes. A dungeon
of pungent horses, sweaty,
sticky, but smooth on the tip
of her tongue. A hint of smoke.

Then plums!
Those sweet plums!

SINGLE MALT

This water rises from granite,
flows over the peat. Heather
gives it a floral, honeyish note.
It's not like the others.

The fisherman swirls liquid amber
in his glass like the finest wine.

Take Talisker. Cuillin lava it is.
Explodes in your mouth. That
fourteen-year-old over there is full
o' seaweed and salt, ocean air on the nose.

He nods toward a bottle
resting against the window.
Ever hear a Silkie cry?
He throws back his head,
empties the glass.
Like the wind out there.
Lonely it is, this place.
Foggy sobbings, tantrum seas.
Stormin' Skye's style, you know.

He slowly rises. Craggy hands
lift bottle from sill.

A winter warmer they call this stuff. Volcanoes
in the throat. A wee dram'll get ya through.
The soil affects the water, ya see.
The peat's character. Go to Islay,
you'll get another whiskey yet.

He pours a thin stream into his glass,
turns it toward the lamp.
The color turns a strange yellow-brown.

I heard it once, I did. A scream.
Black pounding against dark cliffs.
She showed me the nest site. Last one
seen on Skye. Near Storr. 1916.
A mere lass, she was. I swear
it sounded like a Silkie. If she were here,
she'd agree. No one knows or cares these days.
The sea eagles flew north. Gone with the seal folk.
Forever, we thought.

He squints. Leans forward.
Nay, not a scream. Not even a moan.
A knowin' it was. The birds will find us again.
They will, she said. They'll come home to Skye.

He closes his eyes. Lowers the glass.
The scotch appears golden now, against
his blue sweater.
His voice is distant, like a dream.
There's never a thing lost forever,
that's what she'd say.
I see her at night, you know.
She comes over the ragged banks.
Stay with me, I beg. It's been so long
since I've kissed her face.

He takes a long sip.
Clears his throat.
Aye, a touch of sun she is, on my lips.

MEETING A BOY ON A TRAIN ACROSS COUNTRY

Mammoth engines roar, hiss,
exhale like dragons spitting bursts of steam.
The fiery mouth opens. We step inside,
sneak away from parents,
dare each other to straddle
the undulating links between cars.
We gather train pillows, blankets.
Camp in the vista-dome.
Castanet tracks pull us through
lightning-bleached deserts, red-rock canyons,
windswept fields. All around us,
power spikes, electrifies our lips
as we press them
against cold windows. Rivulets of breath
pool onto metal-encased sills.
The machine's immensity
makes us feel invincible.

Almost
in love.

BALANCE

We dissolve into each other,
sharing routines day after day,
year after year. He says it's like sinking
quietly into the earth while watching
an owl flush from the woods.
Words like these reveal his velvet places.

We minuet around each other in the kitchen,
curse when we disagree, wear apologies on our faces.
He says there's a strong balance
between skill and common sense
while carving a slow arc in the snow.
Words like these echo his instincts.

He digs shards of glass from our favorite beach,
adds them to the razor-sharp piles
already severing his pockets.
What the hell is going on here?
Words like these declare his breaking points.

He pulls embroidery thread from a drawer beside the bed,
mends his jacket with red ladybugs that brag
about how many white dots they wear on their wings,
and adds a swarm of yellow bees sporting broad black stripes.

Balance is like this.
We hold each other's tears.
We reflect each other's smiles.
We sit beneath our favorite tree and listen
for the whispered winging of owls.

FRIENDSHIP CEREMONY

1.
Three lead me out of the storm
and into a sheltered area.
I close my eyes when they blindfold me.
A woman is not allowed
to look upon an eagle feather.
Their words are gentle,
like the falling snow outside.

2.
Three dance around me with sage smoke.
Tee-gupl-mah'wee.
I don't recognize the lyrics of the song.
Their voices hypnotize me into a dream
of stories reeling before a distant fire.
Ancient stories with faces
coming alive in the glow.
Tee-gupl-mah'wee.
The song undulates. Summons
the Gray Hawk. The One Who Travels Far.
Wings circle my neck.
The Gray Hawk. Seldom Seen.
Comes Only When the Lake Calls His Name.
Tee-gupl-mah'wee.
His spotted wings
hold me,
hold me.
Then they let go.

3.
The reception room is too bright.
I squint my eyes.
People sit in chairs at tables,
watching me.
Elders. Children. Friends.
The Tribal Leader.
I discover the pendant around my neck.
Four Gray Hawks, one for each direction,
each season, each cycle of being.
Three elements of Washo life:
Earth. Sun. Water.
Intricately beaded on the medallion
like constellations in a moonless sky.

4.
The aroma of Indian tacos fills the great hall.
Pine Nut Soup. Gray Seed Soup. Medicine Tea.
The Tribal Leader stands, his eyes,
like the Gray Hawk's,
penetrate mine.

Stay good, he says.
Just
stay
good.

ANOTHER SENTIMENTAL LOVE POEM

I love you
as you invite the winter storm into the house,
stomping snow from your boots
on the rug by the door.

As you drop your bags and fall to your knees
before the dog, I love you. As you bury
your head into her neck, mimicking
her muffled songs,

I love you
as you roll to your side, rise
from the floor, groan just a little.
As you silently limp to the kitchen,

I love you as you fill the teakettle,
select a mug, turn up the burner, the radio.
When you finally remove your dripping jacket,
place gloves on the hearth, unlace boots,

add soaked socks and hat to the pile,
I still love you
as you climb the stairs,
return with slippers,

drugstore glasses in your hands.
After you've opened your book
and settled on the couch,
coffee table beneath your feet,

I've loved you so much
I can go back
to my work
and not let on.

Snake Weaver

No one bothers her here
on the edge of town.
She boils her roots and plants her seeds
away from the starched community.

On the edge of town
Snake weaves through her baskets.
Away from the starched community,
she splits her willows and sings her songs.

Snake weaves through her baskets.
He watches her awl lace threads.
She splits her willows and sings her songs.
Shadows move.

He watches her awl lace threads
through silent spaces
where shadows move
toward the edge of town.

Through silent spaces,
Snake slips into darkness
toward the edge of town.
She hums the serpent's song.

Snake slips into darkness.
She boils her roots and plants her seeds.
Hums the serpent's song.
No one bothers her here.

LIGHT LIKE THIS
after Rumi

The splash of sunlight on your face?
That same light just touched the leftovers
a bear scattered in the snow last night. That's not all.
A few minutes ago, it defined a plastic bag
tangled in the willows. Made it shimmer like silver.
Before that, it caught the chrome of a Shelby
humming down Highway 89 toward Sierraville,
blinded the eyes of a hitchhiker sitting on his duffle bag,
vaulted off a crushed beer can, tickled a chickadee's tail,
and waltzed across the lake. If you follow it back
to the moment it crested the mountain, that was when
it grazed the edge of the crystal hanging in the window
near the bird feeders outside. Sent millions of rainbows
dancing through the bedroom
until one finally hit your face.
I kissed the yellow-green
on your cheek.
Remember?

NOTES

- "The Move" and "Rivers" are poems about our previous home at the base of Echo Summit in Meyers, California, before our move to Truckee in 1988.
- "His Cigarette Voice Burns Holes Through Fog" is for Floyd Salas, a flamboyant writer and social activist whom I met when he conducted a poetry workshop at a California Arts Council retreat in the early 1990s. I heard his voice while passing by his classroom and wandered in. "You're late!" he screamed, motioning me to sit in the front row. He scared me to death— until I realized what a great teacher he was.
- While visualizing an extended family living in the world's smallest house in Derbyshire, England, I wrote "Thimble Hall: A Daydream."
- The spelling of "Washo" in "Washo Country" comes from twentieth-century literature I received at invitational gatherings. "Washoe" is the official spelling used by the People today.
- The book that inspired "Grimm" is *Tea with the Black Dragon* by R.A. MacAvoy.

- "See This Mountain?" refers to Cave Rock on the southeastern shore of Lake Tahoe. It remains a sacred site for the Washoe People. After years of contentious court battles, the U.S. Forest Service declared it off-limits to rock climbers. Today, the Washoe continue their work to heal this revered place.
- "Thirty-Seven Days" and "Polling Place" refer to the 2016 presidential election.
- I wrote "Wednesday" in response to the 1999 Columbine High School massacre.
- I pulled "Split" from a pile of poems I'd drafted long ago. I'm not sure what inspired me to write it. A news story? A movie? I decided to include it in this collection because it resonates with the many ways a gun can be used as a metaphor for what triggers us.
- "Eleven Guides" honors the actual birds and animals who accompanied me on a walk as I tried to process the state of the world.
- Midnight musings about the explosive population growth in Truckee inspired "Controlled Growth."
- "My Cousin and Ira Glass" references the host and producer of *This American Life*, a weekly public radio program.
- "Taken By Water" begins with a dream our close friend had while he and his wife were on vacation. The following morning, they were told about the drowning of his schoolmate, Dugald Bremner, in a kayaking accident in 1997.
- After sharing lunch with a troupe of African dancers and storytellers at another California Arts Council retreat in the early 1990s, I escaped to my room and wrote "Surrender."
- "Bremen" is for a beautifully kind and gentle exchange student who asked me to marry him.

- My high school sweetheart told me his last name meant "Of the Wild Horses" in Dutch. After our amicable divorce (and with his blessing), I've continued to sign my artwork with this name. "Feline" and "hee" in the poem refer to my middle nickname, Cathee.
- In "The Wrong Muse," I mentioned David Bohm, a theoretical physicist who has enormously impacted my life, especially concerning the unifying power of supportive dialogue.
- I often engage in imaginative role-playing while writing poetry. "Mrs. Dumpty After the Accident" is an example.
- A bottle of whisky, a midnight encounter with a fisherman on the Isle of Skye, Duncan Williamson's silkie stories, and *The Stoner Eagles* by William Horwood inspired "Single Malt."
- I wrote "Snakeweaver" using a poetic form called a pantoum. It consists of non-rhyming, four-line stanzas creating a pattern of repetitive lines, where the first line of each subsequent stanza is a repeat of the second line in the previous stanza, and the third line of the new stanza is a repeat of the fourth line in the previous stanza. The second and fourth lines of each new stanza are lines that have not been repeated before but come back as the first and third lines of the following stanza. Confusing? Yes. Fun? Absolutely.
- "Friendship Ceremony" is for Yetta, Brian Wallace, the late Darriel Bender—and Al Gore, who agreed to meet with Washoe tribal leaders and elders after receiving "Remembering the Sacred," a card I painted with permission to honor the Washoe People.

THANK YOU

Thank you, Jean Fournier, for helping me select, arrange, and edit this collection.

Thank you, Jibboom Street Writers and Corner Booth Writers, for launching me on this transformative journey.

Thank you, Duncan Muffett, for supporting my poetic efforts over the years.

Thank you to my family, friends, and mentors for inspiring me.

Thank you, Reina Markheim, for acquiring "Dreamtime" and endorsing the use of its image on the cover.

Thank you, Yetta, for your teachings.

Thank you, Greig, for being my most important muse.

Above all, thank you to the forests, mountains, lakes, flora, and all the furry and feathered creatures of the Sierra for allowing me to live here. And, with all my heart, to the Washoe People.

ABOUT THE AUTHOR

M.C. St.Clair is a night owl, wee-hour scribbler, oral storyteller, and an alumna of the Community of Writers in Olympic Valley, California. She lives in Truckee with her husband, Greig, and their special-needs border collie. This is her first book of poetry.

As an artist, she is known as Cathee vanRossem-St.Clair, who has earned national recognition for her paintings on unique surfaces, including eggshells, dream boxes, and rocks her dog drops at her feet. One of her creations, commissioned by the White House, is now in the National Archives.

You can view her work at www.catheestclair.com

ALSO BY M.C. ST.CLAIR

MATING HABITS OF FIREFLIES, A NOVEL

AVAILABLE THROUGH AMAZON.COM

Made in the USA
Columbia, SC
29 July 2024